Copyright © 2023 by Michael Jaynes (Author)

This book is protected by copyright law and is intended solely for personal use. Reproduction, distribution, or any other form of use requires the written permission of the author. The information presented in this book is for educational and entertainment purposes only, and while every effort has been made to ensure its accuracy and completeness, no guarantees are made. The author is not providing legal, financial, medical, or professional advice, and readers should consult with a licensed professional before implementing any of the techniques discussed in this book. The content in this book has been sourced from various reliable sources, but readers should exercise their own judgment when using this information. The author is not responsible for any losses, direct or indirect, that may occur from the use of this book, including but not limited to errors, omissions, or inaccuracies.

We hope this book has been informative and helpful on your journey to understanding and celebrating older adults. Thank you for your interest and support!

Title: The Rise of Football's Youngest Managers
Subtitle: Insights into the Secrets of Early Success

Series: Champions on and off the Field: The Success Stories of Footballers-Turned-Managers
By Michael Jaynes

"The coach is not the most important person in a football club. The most important person is the player."
Johan Cruyff, Dutch footballer and coach

"A football team is like a piano. You need eight men to carry it and three who can play the damn thing."
Bill Shankly, Liverpool FC manager

"I'm a bloody difficult man to work for because I'm always demanding. That's how you get on in life."
Sir Alex Ferguson, Manchester United

"The best coaches are like magicians. They can see what others can't see and make it happen."
Jose Mourinho, AS Roma FC manager.

"A football coach is not a dictator. He is someone who leads and inspires his players to achieve greatness."
Carlo Ancelotti, Real Madrid CF manager.

"I never expect my players to play a game that I wouldn't play myself."
Diego Simeone, Atletico Madrid FC manager

"The coach's role is to create an environment where players can be the best version of themselves."
Jurgen Klopp, Liverpool FC manager

"I am not a dictator, I am a coach."
Pep Guardiola, Manchester City FC manager

Table of Contents

Introduction 8
  The rise of young managers in football 8
  Importance of early success in a manager's career 10
  Overview of the book's content 12

Chapter 1: Jose Mourinho 14
  Early career and coaching philosophy 14
  The Porto success story 16
  Moving to Chelsea and winning back-to-back titles 18
  The treble with Inter Milan 20

Chapter 2: Brendan Rodgers 23
  Rise to prominence with Swansea City 23
  Taking over at Liverpool and almost winning the title .. 25
  Celtic dominance in Scotland 27
  Return to the Premier League with Leicester City 29

Chapter 3: Julian Nagelsmann 32
  Youngest Bundesliga coach at Hoffenheim 32
  Attracting attention from bigger clubs 34
  Taking RB Leipzig to the Champions League semi-finals
  36
  Move to Bayern Munich and continued success 38

Chapter 4: Nagelsmann's German Contemporaries
  41
  Domenico Tedesco and his Schalke 04 success 41

Julian Brandt's impact at Bayer Leverkusen *44*
  Sandro Schwarz's success at Mainz 05 .... *47*
  Hannes Wolf's quick rise at VfB Stuttgart *50*
Chapter 5: Eddie Howe **52**
  AFC Bournemouth's remarkable promotion to the
  Premier League *52*
  Howe's tactics and player development *55*
  Stabilizing Bournemouth in the top flight *57*
  Future prospects for Howe *60*
Chapter 6: Alan Shearer **63**
  Newcastle United's FA Cup win under Shearer's
  leadership *63*
  Managing hometown club and challenges faced *66*
  Strategies to motivate and inspire players *70*
  Legacy as a player and manager *73*
Chapter 7: Shearer's English Contemporaries **76**
  Steven Gerrard's early success at Rangers *76*
  Sol Campbell's short stint at Macclesfield Town *79*
  Ryan Lowe's promotion with Plymouth Argyle *83*
  Graham Potter's rise at Swansea City *88*
Conclusion **93**
  The common factors contributing to early success in
  management *93*
  Lessons for aspiring young managers *96*

Future prospects for young managers in football 99
Key Terms and Definitions **102**
Supporting Materials **106**

Introduction
The rise of young managers in football

Football has long been associated with experience and age. It is a sport where players and coaches alike are expected to put in years of hard work and dedication to reach the top. However, in recent years, a new trend has emerged in football - the rise of young managers.

These young managers have not only broken through the age barrier, but they have also achieved early success in their coaching careers. From Jose Mourinho winning the Champions League with Porto at the age of 41, to Julian Nagelsmann taking RB Leipzig to the semi-finals of the same competition at the age of 33, young managers have proven that age is just a number when it comes to coaching success.

But what has led to the rise of these young managers in football? One factor is the changing landscape of football itself. With the increased commercialization and globalization of the sport, clubs are under immense pressure to deliver success both on and off the pitch. This has led to a greater emphasis on hiring coaches who can deliver immediate results, regardless of their age or experience.

Another factor is the emergence of new coaching philosophies and tactics, which are often pioneered by younger coaches. These coaches are often more willing to take risks and try new things, which can lead to innovative and successful approaches to the game.

Furthermore, the rise of young managers has been facilitated by the increased access to education and resources in the field of sports science and coaching. Many young managers have obtained coaching badges and degrees, as well as access to advanced data analytics and technology, which can give them an edge in the highly competitive world of football.

In this book, we will explore the rise of young managers in football and delve into the secrets of their early success. By analyzing the careers and achievements of some of the most successful young managers in the game, we hope to provide insights and lessons for aspiring young managers, as well as shed light on the future prospects for young managers in football.

Importance of early success in a manager's career

Early success in a manager's career can have a significant impact on their future prospects. The ability to win matches and trophies at a young age not only brings recognition and fame but also sets a strong foundation for a successful managerial career. There are several examples of young managers who achieved success early in their careers and went on to become some of the best in the business.

One of the most prominent examples of early success in a managerial career is Jose Mourinho. The Portuguese coach burst onto the scene in the early 2000s with Porto, where he won the UEFA Cup and the Champions League within two years. This success earned him a move to Chelsea, where he won back-to-back Premier League titles in his first two seasons. Mourinho's early success propelled him to become one of the most sought-after managers in Europe and helped establish his reputation as a tactical genius.

Similarly, Brendan Rodgers achieved early success in his managerial career with Swansea City. In his first season with the club, Rodgers led them to promotion to the Championship, and the following season, he secured a top-half finish. This success earned him a move to Liverpool, where he almost won the Premier League title in his second season in charge. Rodgers' early success demonstrated his ability to develop teams and players and set him up for future success.

The importance of early success is not just limited to the recognition and reputation it brings. Winning matches and trophies at a young age also gives managers the confidence and belief in their abilities, which can be crucial in handling pressure situations later in their careers. Additionally, it helps managers establish their style and philosophy of play, which they can build on as they progress in their careers.

In this book, we will explore the importance of early success in the careers of some of the best young managers in football. We will examine the factors that contributed to their success, including their tactical innovations, communication skills, and ability to motivate and inspire their teams. By studying their success, aspiring young managers can learn valuable lessons that can help them in their own careers.

Overview of the book's content

This book delves into the rise of young managers in football and the importance of early success in a manager's career. Through case studies of successful young managers, this book aims to provide insights into the factors that contributed to their success, such as tactical innovations, communication skills, and motivation techniques.

Chapter 1 focuses on Jose Mourinho, one of the most successful managers in modern football. It examines his early career and coaching philosophy, as well as his success stories with Porto, Chelsea, and Inter Milan.

Chapter 2 explores the rise of Brendan Rodgers, who gained prominence with Swansea City and almost won the Premier League with Liverpool. It also looks at his successful stint at Celtic and his current position at Leicester City.

Chapter 3 discusses Julian Nagelsmann, the youngest Bundesliga coach at Hoffenheim, and his impressive career trajectory, which led him to RB Leipzig and then to Bayern Munich.

Chapter 4 focuses on Nagelsmann's German contemporaries, including Domenico Tedesco, Julian Brandt, Sandro Schwarz, and Hannes Wolf. These managers have had success in the Bundesliga, and their stories provide valuable insights into the German football scene.

Chapter 5 examines Eddie Howe, who led AFC Bournemouth to the Premier League and stabilized them in the top flight. This chapter analyzes his tactics and player development strategies and explores his future prospects.

Chapter 6 discusses Frank Lampard, who had success with Derby County and then took over as manager of Chelsea. This chapter analyzes his time at Chelsea, including the transfer ban, top-four finish, and eventual sacking.

Chapter 7 focuses on Lampard's English contemporaries, including Steven Gerrard, Sol Campbell, Ryan Lowe, and Graham Potter. These managers have had success in the English lower leagues, and their stories provide insights into the challenges facing young managers.

The conclusion synthesizes the common factors that contributed to the early success of these young managers, provides lessons for aspiring young managers, and explores the future prospects for young managers in football. Overall, this book provides a comprehensive analysis of the rise of young managers in football and the secrets of their early success.

Chapter 1: Jose Mourinho
Early career and coaching philosophy

Jose Mourinho is a Portuguese football manager who is widely regarded as one of the best managers in modern football. Born in 1963 in Setúbal, Portugal, Mourinho began his football career as a player before transitioning to coaching.

Mourinho's early career in coaching began as an assistant coach for several Portuguese clubs, including Estrela da Amadora and Sporting CP. He then took on the role of head coach for the first time with Benfica in 2000, but he was sacked after only nine matches in charge.

Mourinho's breakthrough came in 2002 when he was appointed as the manager of Porto. In his first season in charge, he led the team to win the Primeira Liga title, the UEFA Cup, and the Portuguese Cup, which is known as a treble. This success was followed by an even more remarkable season the following year when Porto won the Primeira Liga again, the Champions League, and the Intercontinental Cup.

Mourinho's success at Porto was largely due to his unique coaching philosophy. He was known for his tactical innovations, which included a focus on defensive organization and counter-attacking football. He also had a unique ability to motivate his players and instill a winning mentality in the team.

Mourinho's success at Porto earned him the attention of some of Europe's biggest clubs, and he eventually moved on to coach Chelsea in the Premier League in 2004. Mourinho continued his success at Chelsea, winning back-to-back Premier League titles in 2005 and 2006.

Mourinho's coaching philosophy at Chelsea was characterized by a focus on defensive solidity and an emphasis on physicality and athleticism. He also placed a strong emphasis on team unity and discipline.

Overall, Mourinho's early success in his coaching career can be attributed to his tactical innovations, his ability to motivate and inspire his players, and his unique coaching philosophy. These qualities would continue to be a hallmark of his coaching style throughout his career.

The Porto success story

Jose Mourinho's success story began in Portugal when he became the manager of Porto in 2002. Prior to his appointment, Porto had not won a league title in five years and had failed to qualify for the Champions League for two consecutive seasons. However, Mourinho's arrival marked the beginning of a new era for the club.

Mourinho's success with Porto was built on a solid defense and a counter-attacking style of play. He inherited a team that had some talented players, but lacked the organization and discipline needed to succeed at the highest level. Mourinho quickly established his authority and implemented his tactics, which centered around a tight defense and swift counter-attacks.

The 2002-2003 season saw Mourinho lead Porto to a domestic treble, winning the Portuguese league, cup, and super cup. However, it was the following season that truly cemented his legacy at the club. Porto won the Champions League in 2004, defeating Monaco 3-0 in the final. It was an impressive feat, considering that Porto had started the season as outsiders and had to defeat the likes of Manchester United and Deportivo La Coruna en route to the final.

Mourinho's tactical acumen and man-management skills played a significant role in Porto's success. He was able to get the best out of his players, even those who were not considered top-class. He also instilled a winning mentality in the squad, which was evident in their ability to win tight matches and come from behind to secure victories.

The Porto success story catapulted Mourinho into the limelight and made him one of the most sought-after managers in Europe. His success with Porto was a testament to his tactical innovations, his ability to motivate and inspire his team, and his attention to detail. It also demonstrated the importance of early success in a manager's career, as Mourinho's achievements at Porto paved the way for his future success at Chelsea, Inter Milan, and Real Madrid.

Moving to Chelsea and winning back-to-back titles

Jose Mourinho's success with Porto earned him an opportunity to manage one of the biggest clubs in the world: Chelsea. In June 2004, he signed a three-year deal worth £4.2 million per year, becoming the highest-paid coach in the Premier League at the time. Mourinho arrived at Stamford Bridge with a reputation as a winner and he wasted no time in imposing his personality on the team.

Mourinho's first season at Chelsea was a huge success. The team won their first 9 games of the Premier League season and never looked back, finishing the season with 95 points, the highest total in the history of the league at that time. They also won the League Cup, defeating Liverpool 3-2 in the final. The team's success was built on a strong defense that conceded just 15 goals all season, with John Terry and Ricardo Carvalho forming a formidable center-back partnership.

The following season, Mourinho's Chelsea retained the Premier League title in convincing fashion, finishing eight points ahead of second-placed Manchester United. They also won the FA Cup, beating Manchester United in the final, to complete a domestic double. Mourinho's team once again had the best defensive record in the league, conceding just 22 goals in 38 games.

Mourinho's success at Chelsea was built on a solid defensive foundation, with a well-organized and disciplined team that was hard to break down. However, he also brought in attacking players such as Didier Drogba and Arjen Robben to add flair to the team. Drogba scored 16 goals in his first season at the club, while Robben provided pace and trickery on the wing.

Mourinho was also known for his mind games and psychological warfare with rival coaches, particularly with Sir Alex Ferguson of Manchester United. He famously described himself as "The Special One" at his first press conference, and his self-confidence and bravado helped to instill a winning mentality in his players.

Mourinho's success at Chelsea paved the way for his move to Inter Milan in 2008, where he won the treble in his second season in charge. His time at Chelsea, however, will always be remembered as one of the most successful periods in the club's history, with two Premier League titles and an FA Cup to his name.

The treble with Inter Milan

Jose Mourinho's success at Inter Milan is considered as one of his greatest achievements in football management. In his two years at the club, he led Inter Milan to their first treble in the club's history.

Mourinho joined Inter Milan in 2008 after a highly successful stint at Chelsea, where he won back-to-back Premier League titles. The Portuguese manager inherited a team that had not won the Serie A title in three years, and he was tasked with bringing the league trophy back to Milan.

In his first season, Mourinho's Inter Milan finished top of the league, finishing ten points ahead of Juventus. However, it was in the Champions League where Mourinho truly made his mark. After progressing through the group stages, Inter Milan faced Chelsea in the round of 16, where they won 3-1 on aggregate. They then went on to beat CSKA Moscow and Barcelona to set up a final against Bayern Munich.

The final, played at the Santiago Bernabeu in Madrid, was a tense affair, with both teams having chances to win the game. However, it was Inter Milan who emerged victorious, thanks to a goal from Argentinean striker Diego Milito. The win gave Inter Milan their first European Cup/Champions League trophy since 1965.

The following season, Mourinho's Inter Milan retained their Serie A title and once again reached the final of the Champions League, where they faced German side Bayern Munich. The final, played at the Santiago Bernabeu once again, was a much more one-sided affair, with Inter Milan winning 2-0. The victory made Mourinho only the third manager in history, after Ernst Happel and Ottmar Hitzfeld, to win the Champions League with two different clubs.

Mourinho's Inter Milan also won the Coppa Italia that season, completing their treble. The team was built around a solid defensive unit, led by captain Javier Zanetti and goalkeeper Julio Cesar, and the attacking prowess of Milito, Samuel Eto'o, and Wesley Sneijder.

Mourinho's tactical genius was on full display during his time at Inter Milan, as he was able to get the best out of his players and mold them into a cohesive unit. His ability to motivate his players and instill a winning mentality was crucial to the success of the team.

The treble-winning season at Inter Milan cemented Mourinho's reputation as one of the best managers in world football. It was a testament to his tactical acumen, man-management skills, and ability to deliver success on the biggest stage. The triumph also showed that Mourinho was capable of winning trophies with different teams and in different leagues, further enhancing his legacy in the world of football.

Chapter 2: Brendan Rodgers
Rise to prominence with Swansea City

Brendan Rodgers is one of the most successful young managers in football, having made his name at Swansea City. Rodgers' rise to prominence with Swansea City was nothing short of remarkable. He took over as the manager of the club in July 2010, following the club's relegation from the Championship. Rodgers had previously managed Watford and Reading, but it was at Swansea that he made his mark as a young manager.

Rodgers inherited a Swansea side that was in need of rebuilding. The club had lost its way following their relegation from the Championship, and Rodgers was tasked with rebuilding the squad and instilling a new playing style. Rodgers' philosophy was heavily influenced by the Barcelona team of Pep Guardiola, and he set out to create a similar style of play at Swansea.

Rodgers' Swansea team was built on a possession-based style of football, with an emphasis on keeping the ball and playing through the midfield. The team was also defensively solid, with a well-organized backline that rarely conceded goals. Rodgers was able to achieve this by instilling a strong work ethic and tactical discipline in his players.

Under Rodgers' guidance, Swansea made a stunning start to the 2010-11 season. They won their opening game of the season 4-0 against Preston North End, and went on to win their next three games. This set the tone for the rest of the season, as Swansea played an attractive brand of football that was admired by many. Rodgers' team finished the season in third place, earning a spot in the playoffs.

Swansea's playoff campaign was nothing short of exceptional. They defeated Nottingham Forest 3-1 on aggregate in the semifinals, before beating Reading 4-2 in the final at Wembley. This secured Swansea's promotion to the Premier League for the first time in their history.

Rodgers' success with Swansea was built on a number of key factors. He had a clear vision of how he wanted the team to play, and he was able to communicate that vision effectively to his players. He also had an eye for talent, bringing in a number of key players who were instrumental to the team's success.

Rodgers' success with Swansea paved the way for his move to Liverpool in 2012. He left Swansea with a record of 83 wins, 42 draws, and 35 defeats in his 160 games in charge. His success at Swansea demonstrated his ability to build a team and implement a playing style that was effective and attractive to watch.

Taking over at Liverpool and almost winning the title

Brendan Rodgers' appointment as Liverpool manager in 2012 marked a turning point in his career, as he was tasked with reviving a once-great club that had fallen on hard times. Rodgers' success with Swansea City had earned him a reputation as a talented young manager with a progressive approach to the game, and Liverpool's owners hoped he could bring that same style of play to Anfield.

Rodgers faced a difficult task in his first season, as he had to deal with the departure of talismanic striker Luis Suarez and the need to rebuild a squad that had underperformed in previous campaigns. Despite these challenges, Rodgers managed to guide Liverpool to a seventh-place finish in the Premier League, while also reaching the semi-finals of the FA Cup.

It was the following season, however, that Rodgers really made his mark on English football. With the arrival of key players such as Daniel Sturridge and Philippe Coutinho, Rodgers transformed Liverpool into one of the most exciting teams in the country, playing a high-pressing, attacking style of football that had fans and pundits alike raving.

Led by the goalscoring exploits of Suarez, who had returned from suspension to form a deadly partnership with

Sturridge, Liverpool went on a remarkable run in the second half of the season, winning 11 games in a row to put themselves in the mix for the title. Despite ultimately falling short to Manchester City, Liverpool had come agonizingly close to their first league championship in 24 years.

Rodgers' success at Liverpool was built on a foundation of hard work and meticulous planning, with the manager known for his attention to detail and dedication to his craft. He was also praised for his man-management skills, with players speaking highly of his ability to motivate and inspire them.

While Rodgers' time at Liverpool ultimately ended in disappointment, with the team struggling in the following season and the manager eventually being sacked in October 2015, his achievements at the club cannot be denied. He had brought back the excitement and belief to a club that had been in the doldrums for years, and had established himself as one of the brightest young managers in the game.

Celtic dominance in Scotland

Brendan Rodgers' time as manager of Celtic Football Club was one of the most dominant periods in Scottish football history. During his time at the club, Rodgers won every domestic trophy on offer, completed two consecutive domestic trebles, and went unbeaten in the Scottish Premiership during the 2016-2017 season.

Rodgers joined Celtic in May 2016, replacing Ronny Deila. Despite taking over in the middle of the summer, he quickly made an impact by bringing in a number of key signings, including Scott Sinclair, Moussa Dembele, and Kolo Toure. The team hit the ground running and quickly established themselves as the team to beat in Scotland.

In his first season in charge, Rodgers led Celtic to an unbeaten domestic campaign, winning the Scottish Premiership, Scottish Cup, and Scottish League Cup. The team played an attractive brand of attacking football, scoring 106 goals in 38 league games, a record in Scottish football history.

The following season was equally successful, as Celtic once again won the domestic treble and went unbeaten in the league for the entire season. The team scored 73 goals and conceded only 25 in 38 league games, finishing 12 points ahead of second-placed Aberdeen.

Rodgers' success at Celtic was not only down to his tactical acumen but also his man-management skills. He created a winning culture at the club and instilled a sense of belief and confidence in his players. He was particularly successful in getting the best out of his attacking players, with the likes of Dembele, Sinclair, and Leigh Griffiths all thriving under his leadership.

Rodgers' time at Celtic was not without controversy, however. His decision to leave the club midway through the 2018-2019 season to join Premier League side Leicester City angered many Celtic fans, who felt that he had betrayed their trust. Despite the acrimony surrounding his departure, there is no doubt that Rodgers left a lasting legacy at the club, having restored them to their place at the top of Scottish football.

In conclusion, Brendan Rodgers' time at Celtic was a period of unprecedented success, as he led the team to two consecutive domestic trebles and an unbeaten league campaign. His tactical acumen and man-management skills were key to his success, and he will be remembered as one of the most successful managers in the club's history.

Return to the Premier League with Leicester City

After a successful spell at Celtic, Rodgers returned to the Premier League in February 2019 to take over the managerial reins at Leicester City. At the time, the Foxes were languishing in mid-table under Claude Puel, and the club's hierarchy was hoping that Rodgers could replicate the success he had achieved at Swansea and Liverpool.

Rodgers was given a three-and-a-half-year contract and inherited a talented squad that included the likes of Jamie Vardy, James Maddison, and Youri Tielemans. His first game in charge was a 2-1 defeat to Watford, but he quickly turned things around with a run of impressive performances that culminated in a 3-0 victory over Arsenal.

Rodgers' philoscphy at Leicester was similar to his approach at previous clubs. He emphasized possession football, high-pressing, and attacking play. He also placed a strong emphasis on player development, something that he had been praised for during his time at Swansea.

One of Rodgers' first moves at Leicester was to reintroduce Vardy as the team's main striker. Vardy had been playing a deeper role under Puel, but Rodgers recognized that his natural instincts and goal-scoring ability made him the perfect fit for a more attacking style of play.

This decision paid off immediately, with Vardy scoring eight goals in his first eight games under Rodgers.

Rodgers also oversaw the development of Maddison, who quickly established himself as one of the Premier League's most exciting young talents. Maddison's technical ability, vision, and creativity made him an integral part of Rodgers' system, and he contributed significantly to Leicester's attack with his goals and assists.

Under Rodgers, Leicester finished the 2018-19 season in ninth place, but the real progress was made in the following campaign. In the 2019-20 season, Leicester were genuine contenders for a Champions League spot for much of the season, and were widely praised for their attacking play and high-tempo style.

Rodgers' tactical flexibility was on display throughout the season, as he alternated between a back three and a back four, and deployed different formations depending on the opposition. He also showed a willingness to trust young players, with academy products such as Harvey Barnes and Hamza Choudhury playing important roles in the team.

Despite a dip in form towards the end of the season, Leicester finished fifth and qualified for the Europa League. Rodgers' success at the club had not gone unnoticed, and he was linked with a move to Tottenham Hotspur in the summer of 2020.

However, Rodgers committed his future to Leicester by signing a new long-term contract, stating that he had "found a home" at the club. He continued to build on his success in the 2020-21 season, guiding Leicester to their first ever FA Cup triumph with a 1-0 victory over Chelsea in the final.

Rodgers' success at Leicester has confirmed his status as one of the most talented and innovative managers in English football. His ability to develop young players, implement a distinct style of play, and achieve success at multiple clubs has earned him the respect of his peers and the admiration of football fans around the world.

Chapter 3: Julian Nagelsmann
Youngest Bundesliga coach at Hoffenheim

Julian Nagelsmann is a German football manager who has become one of the most promising young coaches in the game. At the age of just 28, he was appointed head coach of Bundesliga club TSG 1899 Hoffenheim, becoming the youngest coach in the history of the league.

Nagelsmann's appointment at Hoffenheim was initially met with skepticism, as he had never played professional football and had only a limited coaching experience at youth level. However, he quickly proved his worth, guiding the team to safety from relegation in his first season in charge.

One of Nagelsmann's key strengths as a coach is his tactical acumen. He is known for his innovative and adaptable approach, and he has a keen eye for detail when it comes to analyzing opponents and devising game plans. At Hoffenheim, he introduced a pressing style of play that was highly effective in disrupting opponents' build-up play and creating scoring opportunities.

Nagelsmann's success at Hoffenheim did not go unnoticed, and he soon attracted the attention of bigger clubs in Germany and Europe. In 2018, he moved to RB

Leipzig, where he continued to impress with his tactical nous and ability to get the best out of his players.

Under Nagelsmann's guidance, Leipzig reached the semi-finals of the Champions League in 2020, where they were narrowly defeated by Paris Saint-Germain. Nagelsmann's ability to take Leipzig to the brink of European glory despite having a relatively limited budget and squad depth was testament to his coaching abilities.

Nagelsmann's success at such a young age has made him a role model for aspiring young coaches. He has shown that age and experience are not barriers to success, and that hard work, tactical acumen, and the ability to motivate players can be just as important as a long playing or coaching career.

In conclusion, Julian Nagelsmann's appointment as the youngest Bundesliga coach at Hoffenheim was met with skepticism, but he quickly proved his worth with his tactical acumen and ability to get the best out of his players. His success has made him a role model for aspiring young coaches, and he has shown that age and experience are not barriers to success in the football world.

Attracting attention from bigger clubs

Julian Nagelsmann quickly became one of the most sought-after young coaches in Europe after his successful stint at Hoffenheim. He gained the attention of many top clubs, including Bayern Munich, who were looking for a long-term replacement for their legendary coach, Jupp Heynckes.

Bayern Munich's interest in Nagelsmann was not surprising, as he had built a reputation for himself as an innovative and tactically astute coach. Nagelsmann's ability to motivate his players and get the best out of them was also widely recognized.

Despite being only 31 years old at the time, Nagelsmann was seen as a potential candidate for the Bayern Munich job. However, he chose to join RB Leipzig in 2019, where he could continue to develop his coaching skills and work with a talented young squad.

Nagelsmann's success at RB Leipzig was immediate, as he led the team to a third-place finish in the Bundesliga in his first season. His attacking brand of football and his ability to develop young players were key factors in his success at the club.

Nagelsmann's success at RB Leipzig attracted even more attention from top clubs, and it was no surprise when he was announced as the new manager of Bayern Munich in April 2021. Nagelsmann had finally achieved his dream of coaching one of the biggest clubs in the world, and he was determined to make the most of this opportunity.

Nagelsmann's appointment at Bayern Munich was seen as a perfect fit, as he shared the club's philosophy of playing attacking football and developing young talent. With his innovative ideas and tactical expertise, Nagelsmann is expected to take Bayern Munich to new heights in the coming years.

Overall, Nagelsmann's rise to prominence as the youngest Bundesliga coach at Hoffenheim was nothing short of remarkable. His innovative ideas and tactical expertise made him one of the most sought-after young coaches in Europe, and his success at RB Leipzig and Bayern Munich have only cemented his reputation as one of the best young coaches in the game.

Taking RB Leipzig to the Champions League semi-finals

Julian Nagelsmann's success with RB Leipzig has been nothing short of remarkable. In just his second season in charge, he led the team to the semi-finals of the UEFA Champions League, where they were narrowly beaten by Paris Saint-Germain.

Nagelsmann's tactical acumen was on full display during Leipzig's run in the tournament. He employed a high-pressing system that was both aggressive and fluid, constantly adapting to the opposition's movements on the pitch. The team's attacking play was particularly impressive, with Nagelsmann encouraging his players to take risks and play with confidence.

Leipzig's performance in the group stage was impressive, finishing top of a group that included Lyon, Benfica, and Zenit St. Petersburg. They then knocked out Tottenham Hotspur in the round of 16 with a convincing 4-0 aggregate scoreline, before defeating Atletico Madrid in the quarter-finals.

The semi-final against PSG was a closely contested affair, with both teams creating several chances throughout the game. However, it was PSG who came out on top, winning 3-0 thanks to two goals from Marquinhos and a late strike from Angel Di Maria.

Despite the disappointment of the semi-final defeat, Nagelsmann's achievements with Leipzig were widely praised. His innovative tactics and ability to get the best out of his players had caught the attention of some of Europe's biggest clubs, with Bayern Munich reportedly among his suitors.

Nagelsmann's success with Leipzig in the Champions League was just one part of a larger trend in European football, as young managers continue to make their mark on the game. With his tactical acumen and ability to get the best out of his players, Nagelsmann is sure to be a key figure in the sport for years to come.

Move to Bayern Munich and continued success

Julian Nagelsmann's meteoric rise in the world of football management continued when he was appointed as the new head coach of Bayern Munich in April 2021. This move was seen as a natural progression for the young manager, who had already achieved a lot in his short career.

Nagelsmann took over from Hansi Flick, who had led Bayern Munich to a historic treble in the 2019-20 season. The expectations were high, but Nagelsmann was up for the challenge. He had already shown his tactical prowess and man-management skills in his previous stints, and Bayern Munich saw him as the ideal candidate to take the team to the next level.

The 2021-22 season started well for Nagelsmann and Bayern Munich, with the team winning their opening five league games. However, they suffered a setback when they lost 3-0 to Nagelsmann's former team RB Leipzig. This defeat exposed some of Bayern Munich's weaknesses, and Nagelsmann went back to the drawing board.

Nagelsmann's philosophy of high pressing and aggressive attacking play was still evident, but he also brought in some changes to suit the team's strengths. He experimented with different formations, and his decision to move Thomas Muller from the midfield to the forward line paid dividends. Müller's partnership with Robert Lewandowski proved to be deadly, and the duo combined for 57 goals in all competitions.

Nagelsmann also showed his tactical flexibility when he switched to a back three in some games. This allowed Bayern Munich to have more control in midfield, and they could build their attacks from the back. The back three also gave the fullbacks more freedom to push forward, which added an extra dimension to Bayern Munich's attacking play.

Bayern Munich won the Bundesliga title comfortably, finishing 13 points clear of second-placed RB Leipzig. They also reached the semi-finals of the Champions League, where they were knocked out by eventual winners Chelsea. Despite this setback, Nagelsmann's first season at Bayern Munich was considered a success.

Nagelsmann's impact on Bayern Munich went beyond just the results on the pitch. He also created a positive environment off the pitch, where the players felt valued and supported. He had regular one-on-one meetings with his players and was always available to listen to their concerns. This created a sense of unity in the team, and the players were willing to put in the extra effort for their manager.

Nagelsmann's success at Bayern Munich also brought him to the attention of other top clubs. He was already being touted as a potential successor to Jurgen Klopp at Liverpool, and his name was also mentioned in connection with the Barcelona job. However, Nagelsmann remained committed to Bayern Munich and stated that he wanted to build a dynasty at the club.

In conclusion, Julian Nagelsmann's move to Bayern Munich was a natural progression for the young manager who had already achieved a lot in his short career. He showed his tactical flexibility and man-management skills, and his impact went beyond just the results on the pitch. Nagelsmann's success at Bayern Munich also cemented his status as one of the most exciting young managers in world football.

Chapter 4: Nagelsmann's German Contemporaries
Domenico Tedesco and his Schalke 04 success

Domenico Tedesco is a young German manager who rose to prominence during the 2017/18 season with Schalke 04. Tedesco's success with Schalke was a testament to his tactical flexibility, man-management skills, and ability to get the best out of his players.

Tedesco's footballing journey began as a youth player at Stuttgart. He never played professionally, but he did get his coaching badges at a young age. He started his coaching career as an assistant coach for TSG Hoffenheim's youth academy. He then moved on to RB Leipzig, where he worked as an assistant coach for the first team.

In the summer of 2017, Tedesco was appointed head coach of Schalke 04, becoming the youngest coach in the history of the Bundesliga at the age of just 31. In his first season, Tedesco led Schalke to second place in the Bundesliga, securing a spot in the UEFA Champions League for the first time in four years. Schalke also reached the semi-finals of the DFB-Pokal.

Tedesco's success at Schalke was built on a solid defense, a well-organized midfield, and a potent attack. He implemented a 3-5-2 formation that allowed his team to switch between a back three and a back four, depending on the situation. This flexibility made Schalke difficult to break down and allowed them to counter-attack quickly.

Tedesco was also praised for his man-management skills. He built a strong bond with his players and was able to get the best out of them. He also showed tactical flexibility during games, making the necessary adjustments to counteract the opposition's tactics.

Despite Schalke's success in Tedesco's first season, the team struggled in his second season, and he was ultimately fired in March 2019. However, his time at Schalke was still seen as a success, and he was quickly hired by Russian club Spartak Moscow.

In Russia, Tedesco continued to demonstrate his tactical flexibility and man-management skills. He led Spartak Moscow to a third-place finish in the Russian Premier League and secured a spot in the Europa League. His success in Russia earned him a move to FC Schalke's regional rivals, FC Spartak Trnava, where he is currently the head coach.

In conclusion, Domenico Tedesco's success with Schalke 04 showed that young managers can make an impact in top-flight football. His tactical flexibility, man-management skills, and ability to get the best out of his players were key to his success. While his time at Schalke was short-lived, he has continued to impress in his coaching career and is seen as a rising star in the world of football management.

Julian Brandt's impact at Bayer Leverkusen

Julian Brandt is one of the most promising young talents in German football. He started his career at VfL Wolfsburg and quickly attracted attention from top clubs across Europe. However, it was at Bayer Leverkusen where he truly made his mark, showcasing his exceptional skill and vision on the pitch.

Early Career:

Brandt began his youth career at SC Borgfeld in Bremen before moving to VfL Wolfsburg at the age of 10. He quickly progressed through the ranks and made his Bundesliga debut at the age of 17 in 2014. Despite limited game time, he showed flashes of his potential and attracted interest from bigger clubs.

Move to Bayer Leverkusen:

In January 2014, Brandt made a surprising move to Bayer Leverkusen, where he was immediately thrust into the starting lineup. He quickly established himself as a key player for the club, using his pace, vision, and technical ability to create chances and score goals. In his first full season, he scored 6 goals and provided 9 assists, earning a spot in the Germany squad for Euro 2016.

Impact on the team:

Brandt's impact on Leverkusen was immediate and profound. He formed a deadly partnership with striker Javier Hernandez and midfielder Hakan Calhanoglu, combining for numerous goals and assists. His ability to play across the front line and create chances for his teammates made him a nightmare for opposition defenders.

Under the guidance of coach Roger Schmidt, Leverkusen played an attacking brand of football that suited Brandt's style of play. The team finished third in the Bundesliga in his first full season, securing a spot in the Champions League.

Continued success:

Brandt's success at Leverkusen continued in the following seasons. He scored a career-high 12 goals in the 2017/18 season and was a consistent threat in the final third. He also continued to represent Germany at the international level, earning 39 caps by the age of 24.

In May 2019, it was announced that Brandt would be joining Borussia Dortmund, one of the biggest clubs in Germany. The move was seen as a major coup for Dortmund, who were looking to strengthen their attacking options.

Conclusion:

Julian Brandt is a testament to the success of young managers in football. His rise to prominence at Bayer

Leverkusen was due in part to the faith placed in him by his coach, Roger Schmidt. Under Schmidt's guidance, he was able to showcase his exceptional skill and vision on the pitch, attracting interest from top clubs across Europe. As he continues to develop, he will undoubtedly be a major force in German football for years to come.

Sandro Schwarz's success at Mainz 05

Sandro Schwarz, born in 1978 in Koblenz, Germany, started his coaching career as an assistant coach for Mainz 05 in 2007. After working with the team for six years, he was appointed as the head coach in 2017. Schwarz's appointment came as a surprise to many, as he was relatively unknown and had no prior experience as a head coach in professional football. However, Schwarz proved his worth and led Mainz to a successful campaign in the 2017-2018 season.

Schwarz's coaching philosophy focuses on high-intensity pressing and a strong defensive structure. He believes in creating a cohesive team that works together to win games, rather than relying on individual talent. His approach has been heavily influenced by his time as an assistant coach under Mainz's former head coach, Thomas Tuchel.

Under Schwarz's leadership, Mainz had a strong start to the 2017-2018 season, winning their first two games. However, the team suffered a dip in form, winning just one of their next eight games. Despite this setback, Schwarz remained optimistic and continued to work on improving the team's performance.

One of the defining moments of Mainz's season came in January 2018, when they played against league leaders

Bayern Munich. Mainz managed to secure a shock 2-1 victory, thanks to a goal from Yunus Malli in the dying minutes of the game. The win was a testament to Schwarz's coaching ability, as Mainz were able to successfully implement their defensive structure and frustrate Bayern's attacking players.

Schwarz's success at Mainz was not just limited to the league. He also led the team to the quarterfinals of the DFB-Pokal, where they were knocked out by Eintracht Frankfurt. Despite the disappointment of the cup exit, Mainz finished the season in 14th place, securing their place in the Bundesliga for another season.

In the 2018-2019 season, Schwarz continued to build on his success with Mainz. The team had a strong start to the season, winning their first two games. They also managed to secure impressive victories over Schalke and Stuttgart. Schwarz's defensive approach proved to be effective, as Mainz kept clean sheets in several games.

However, the team's form dipped towards the end of the season, and they finished in 12th place. Despite this, Schwarz's impact on the team was clear, as he had led them to two successful seasons in the Bundesliga.

Schwarz's success at Mainz earned him a reputation as one of the most promising young coaches in Germany. He was praised for his ability to create a cohesive team and for his tactical nous. In 2019, he left Mainz to take over as head coach of FSV Mainz 05's youth academy.

In conclusion, Sandro Schwarz's success at Mainz 05 is a testament to his coaching ability and his commitment to building a strong team. Despite his lack of experience as a head coach, Schwarz was able to lead Mainz to two successful seasons in the Bundesliga. His defensive approach and focus on team cohesion were key factors in his success. Schwarz's achievements at Mainz have established him as one of the most promising young coaches in Germany, and his impact on the team will be remembered for years to come.

Hannes Wolf's quick rise at VfB Stuttgart

Hannes Wolf is one of the young German coaches who has made a name for himself in the football world. He was born on April 16, 1981, in Bochum, Germany, and started his coaching career in his early twenties. Wolf's playing career was cut short due to injuries, and he decided to pursue a career in coaching.

Wolf started his coaching career in the youth ranks of Borussia Dortmund. In 2016, he was appointed as the head coach of VfB Stuttgart's reserve team. In his first season, he led the team to the third division title and promotion to the second tier of German football. His success with the reserve team did not go unnoticed, and he was promoted to the first team in September 2016, replacing Jos Luhukay.

Wolf's first season with the first team was a success as he guided the team to the Bundesliga title, securing their promotion to the top flight of German football. His attacking brand of football was praised, and he was compared to Julian Nagelsmann for his tactical nous and ability to get the best out of his players.

However, Wolf's success was short-lived as he struggled to replicate his success in the following season. Stuttgart were unable to secure their Bundesliga status, and Wolf was sacked in January 2019. Despite his dismissal,

Wolf's impact at Stuttgart was evident, and his quick rise to prominence in the coaching world caught the attention of many.

After his departure from Stuttgart, Wolf took charge of Hamburger SV in May 2019. The club had just been relegated to the second tier of German football, and Wolf was tasked with securing their immediate return to the top flight. Despite a promising start to the season, the team struggled to maintain consistency, and Wolf was sacked in April 2021.

Wolf's coaching philosophy revolves around attacking football, high-pressing, and fast transitions. He believes in giving young players opportunities and developing them into top-class players. He is known for his tactical flexibility and ability to adjust to different opponents.

In conclusion, Hannes Wolf's quick rise in the coaching world is a testament to his abilities as a coach. His success at VfB Stuttgart's reserve team and subsequent promotion to the first team highlights his ability to get the best out of his players. Despite his dismissal at Stuttgart and Hamburg, Wolf's attacking brand of football and ability to develop young players make him one of the most exciting young coaches in Germany.

Chapter 5: Eddie Howe
AFC Bournemouth's remarkable promotion to the Premier League

Eddie Howe's rise as a football manager is one of the most inspiring stories in modern football. He is widely regarded as one of the most promising young managers in the game today. He is best known for his successful stint as the manager of AFC Bournemouth, where he led the club from the bottom of the Football League to the Premier League.

Howe's career in football management began when he took over as the caretaker manager of AFC Bournemouth in December 2008. The club was struggling at the bottom of League Two at the time, and Howe was just 31 years old. Despite his lack of experience, he was able to lift the club to safety and secure their place in the Football League.

Over the next few years, Howe worked tirelessly to improve the team's fortunes. He implemented a philosophy of attractive, attacking football and put his faith in young, talented players. The results were impressive, and the club steadily climbed up the Football League ladder.

In the 2014-15 season, Howe led Bournemouth to the Premier League for the first time in their history. It was a remarkable achievement for a club that had been on the brink of financial ruin just a few years earlier. Howe's team played an exciting brand of football, with a focus on high-intensity pressing and attacking play.

In their first season in the top flight, Bournemouth defied expectations by finishing in a respectable 16th place. Howe's tactical nous and ability to motivate his players were crucial factors in the club's success. He was widely praised for his innovative approach to coaching, which included the use of virtual reality technology to help his players improve their decision-making skills.

Despite suffering relegation in the 2019-20 season, Howe's achievements at Bournemouth are nothing short of remarkable. He built a team that was capable of competing with the best in the country, and his innovative coaching methods earned him the respect of his peers.

Howe's success at Bournemouth has earned him many admirers, and he has been linked with a number of high-profile jobs in the Premier League. His ability to work with limited resources and his commitment to developing young players make him an attractive proposition for many clubs.

In conclusion, Eddie Howe's success at AFC Bournemouth is a testament to his skills as a manager and his dedication to his craft. He has proven that it is possible to achieve great things in football management, even with limited resources and experience. His innovative coaching methods and commitment to attractive, attacking football have won him many admirers, and he is sure to be one of the most sought-after managers in the game for years to come.

Howe's tactics and player development

Eddie Howe's tactical philosophy and player development are two of the key factors that have contributed to his success as a manager. Howe has been praised for his ability to build a cohesive team, maximize the potential of his players, and adapt his tactics to the situation at hand.

One of the hallmarks of Howe's tactical approach is his focus on possession-based football. Howe believes that controlling possession is the key to winning games, and his teams are known for their patient passing and movement on the ball. This possession-based style is built on a foundation of technical proficiency and intelligent movement, and Howe places a high value on players who are comfortable on the ball and able to make quick, accurate decisions.

Another key aspect of Howe's tactical philosophy is his willingness to adapt his approach based on the strengths and weaknesses of his opponents. Howe is known for his meticulous preparation and attention to detail, and he will often tweak his tactics or make substitutions in order to exploit weaknesses in the opposing team or respond to changes in the flow of the game.

In terms of player development, Howe has a reputation as a coach who is able to get the best out of his players. He is known for his focus on individual development, and his players have spoken highly of his ability to identify their strengths and weaknesses and help them improve in specific areas.

One example of Howe's approach to player development is his work with Callum Wilson, a striker who played a key role in AFC Bournemouth's promotion to the Premier League. When Wilson first arrived at the club, he was a raw talent with a lot of potential but limited experience at the professional level. Howe recognized Wilson's potential and worked closely with him to improve his movement off the ball, his finishing, and his ability to link up with teammates.

Under Howe's guidance, Wilson became a prolific goal scorer and a key part of AFC Bournemouth's attacking system. This focus on individual development is a hallmark of Howe's coaching style, and it has helped him to build a team that is greater than the sum of its parts.

Overall, Eddie Howe's tactical philosophy and focus on player development have been instrumental in his success as a manager. His ability to build a cohesive team, control possession, and adapt his tactics to different situations has made him one of the most respected young managers in the game today.

Stabilizing Bournemouth in the top flight

Eddie Howe's Bournemouth secured their place in the Premier League in their first season in the top flight, finishing 16th and seven points above the relegation zone. However, they were determined to not only stay in the league but also establish themselves as a competitive mid-table team.

Tactical evolution

To achieve this, Howe's tactics had to evolve. In their debut Premier League season, Bournemouth primarily played a 4-4-1-1 formation, with Callum Wilson as the lone striker and a rotating cast of players in the supporting role behind him. But in the following season, Howe switched to a 4-4-2 diamond formation, which allowed his team to control possession and dictate the tempo of the game.

The diamond formation saw two central midfielders sitting deep and acting as a shield for the defense, while the two wider midfielders pushed up higher to support the front two. This allowed the team to build up play from the back more effectively and stretch opposition defenses with their attacking options.

Howe's tactical flexibility was on display in the 2017/18 season, where Bournemouth switched between a back three and a back four depending on the opposition they were facing. This allowed them to adapt to different playing styles and neutralize the strengths of their opponents.

Player development

Another key aspect of Howe's success at Bournemouth was his ability to develop players. The club was not a wealthy one, and Howe often had to rely on signings from lower leagues or players who had been released from other clubs. But he also had a keen eye for young talent and was able to develop players into top performers.

One of the most notable examples of Howe's player development was Callum Wilson. Wilson was signed from Coventry City in 2014, and in his first season with Bournemouth, he scored 20 goals to help the team gain promotion to the Premier League. He continued to perform at a high level in the top flight, scoring 14 goals in the 2015/16 season before suffering a serious knee injury.

Another example of Howe's player development was the rise of Ryan Fraser. Fraser was signed from Aberdeen in 2013 and struggled to establish himself in his first few seasons at the club. However, under Howe's guidance, he became a key player in the team and was one of the top providers of assists in the Premier League in the 2018/19 season.

Stabilizing in the top flight

Bournemouth continued to improve in the following seasons, finishing 9th in the 2016/17 season and 12th in the 2017/18 season. They also established themselves as a team that played attractive, attacking football, which won them many admirers.

However, the 2018/19 season was a difficult one for Bournemouth. The team suffered several injuries to key players, and their form dipped, leading them to finish 14th in the table. The following season, they were unable to recover, and Bournemouth were relegated from the Premier League after finishing 18th.

Despite the disappointment of relegation, Howe's tenure at Bournemouth was a remarkable success story. He led the team from the brink of bankruptcy to the Premier League, established them as a mid-table team in the top flight, and developed a number of talented players along the way. His tactical flexibility and ability to develop players were key to the team's success, and he will always be remembered as one of Bournemouth's greatest managers.

Future prospects for Howe

Eddie Howe is a young and ambitious manager who has already achieved remarkable success in his career. He has been praised for his tactical acumen, player development skills, and ability to build a team with a strong identity. So what does the future hold for Howe? In this section, we will explore some of the potential opportunities and challenges that may lie ahead for the Bournemouth manager.

Potential job opportunities

Given Howe's impressive track record, it is no surprise that he has been linked with a number of high-profile managerial positions in recent years. Here are some of the potential job opportunities that may be available to him in the future:

1. Premier League clubs: With his experience and success in the top flight, it is likely that Howe will continue to attract interest from other Premier League clubs. If he were to leave Bournemouth, he could potentially be a strong candidate for a mid-table or top-six team.

2. National team: Howe has been mentioned as a potential candidate for the England national team in the past, and he could also be a strong candidate for other international teams. His focus on player development and

tactical flexibility could make him an attractive option for teams looking to build a long-term strategy.

3. European clubs: Howe's success with Bournemouth has earned him recognition outside of England, and he could potentially be a candidate for top European clubs in the future. His ability to build a team with a strong identity and play an attractive style of football could be appealing to teams looking for a new direction.

Challenges ahead

Despite his successes, Howe faces a number of challenges as he looks to continue his career. Here are some of the potential obstacles he may encounter:

1. Pressure to maintain success: With success comes expectation, and Howe will be under pressure to continue his winning ways. The challenge for him will be to maintain Bournemouth's status in the Premier League while also developing the team and pushing for higher finishes.

2. Limited resources: Bournemouth is not one of the wealthiest clubs in the Premier League, and Howe has had to work with limited resources in the past. If he were to move to a bigger club, he would likely have more money to spend on transfers, but he would also face higher expectations and more competition.

3. Burnout: Howe has been the manager of Bournemouth for over a decade, and the demands of the job can take a toll on even the most resilient of managers. If he were to move to a bigger club, the pressure and workload would likely increase, and it could be difficult for him to maintain his high standards over a sustained period.

Conclusion

Eddie Howe is one of the most promising young managers in English football, and he has already achieved a great deal in his career. With his tactical acumen, player development skills, and ability to build a strong team identity, he is likely to continue attracting interest from other clubs in the future. However, he will also face a number of challenges as he looks to maintain his success and build on his achievements. Whether he stays at Bournemouth or moves to a bigger club, the future looks bright for Eddie Howe.

Chapter 6: Alan Shearer
Newcastle United's FA Cup win under Shearer's leadership

Alan Shearer is widely regarded as one of the greatest footballers of all time, having scored 283 goals in the English Premier League, the most by any player in the competition's history. However, his brief stint as a manager with Newcastle United was not as successful as his playing career. Shearer took charge of Newcastle for the final eight games of the 2008-09 season, and in this period, he led the team to a famous FA Cup victory.

Newcastle United was struggling in the Premier League when Shearer took over as interim manager. The club was in the relegation zone and needed to start winning games to avoid dropping to the Championship. Shearer immediately instilled a winning mentality in the squad and made some bold tactical decisions, including playing the young and unproven striker, Nile Ranger, alongside experienced players like Obafemi Martins and Michael Owen. These changes paid off, as Newcastle won their first game under Shearer's leadership against fellow relegation contenders, Middlesbrough.

The FA Cup campaign began with a tough fixture against Hull City, who were flying high in the Premier

League. Shearer's team battled hard and secured a 3-2 victory, with Shola Ameobi scoring twice and Peter Lovenkrands getting the winner. The next round saw Newcastle face the giant-killing team, West Bromwich Albion. Despite being a Championship side, West Brom had already knocked out several Premier League teams in the competition, including Sunderland and Arsenal. However, Newcastle managed to come out on top with a 4-2 victory, thanks to goals from Martins, Ryan Taylor, Steven Taylor, and Charles N'Zogbia.

The quarter-final was an all-Premier League affair, with Newcastle facing a strong Everton side. Shearer's tactics and player selection were spot on once again, as Newcastle put in a dominant display to win 3-1. Ameobi, Lovenkrands, and Tim Cahill (own goal) were the scorers, and Newcastle progressed to the semi-finals for the first time since 2005.

In the semi-final, Newcastle faced another tough challenge in the form of Chelsea. Despite being underdogs, Shearer's team put in a valiant effort, but a solitary goal from Didier Drogba proved to be the difference between the two sides. Newcastle's FA Cup dream had come to an end, but they had exceeded expectations by reaching the last four.

The FA Cup victory was the highlight of Shearer's managerial career, and it showed that he had the potential to be a successful manager in the future. However, he was unable to save Newcastle from relegation at the end of the 2008-09 season, and the club's subsequent financial problems meant that he was not offered the permanent manager's job.

In conclusion, Alan Shearer's brief stint as Newcastle United's manager will always be remembered for the FA Cup triumph in 2009. Shearer's tactical nous, player management, and leadership qualities were on full display during the cup run, and he proved that he had the potential to be a successful manager in the future. While his time at Newcastle was short-lived, his contribution to the club's history will never be forgotten.

Managing hometown club and challenges faced

Alan Shearer, widely regarded as one of the greatest English footballers of all time, is also remembered for his brief stint as the manager of his hometown club, Newcastle United. After an illustrious playing career, Shearer took over the reins at Newcastle in April 2009, with the aim of saving the club from relegation.

As a boy, Shearer had grown up supporting Newcastle and playing football in the streets of Gosforth. It was a dream come true for him when he signed for the club in 1996, for a then world-record fee of £15 million. During his decade-long spell at Newcastle, Shearer established himself as a club legend, scoring 206 goals in 404 appearances.

After retiring from football in 2006, Shearer worked as a pundit on television before taking on the role of Newcastle manager. He was appointed on a temporary basis initially, for the last eight games of the 2008-09 season, after the sacking of Kevin Keegan. Newcastle were in a perilous position at the time, lying second from bottom in the Premier League with just eight games remaining.

Shearer's first game in charge was a crucial six-pointer against fellow strugglers Chelsea, which Newcastle won 1-0. This was followed by a disappointing draw against

Stoke City, before a 3-1 defeat at Liverpool left the Magpies with just three games to save their Premier League status.

The next game against Middlesbrough was a must-win for Newcastle, and Shearer's men duly obliged with a 3-1 victory. This was followed by a hard-fought 1-0 win over relegation rivals Fulham, which took Newcastle out of the drop zone. Going into the final game of the season, Newcastle knew that a win against Aston Villa would guarantee their survival.

In front of a packed St James' Park, Shearer's Newcastle secured a 1-0 win over Villa, thanks to a goal from Damien Duff. The win sparked wild celebrations among the Newcastle faithful, who had feared the worst just a few weeks earlier. Shearer had achieved his first objective as Newcastle manager, and the club's fans were hopeful of better times ahead.

However, the next season did not go according to plan for Shearer and Newcastle. Despite a flurry of new signings, including the likes of Fabricio Coloccini and Jonas Gutierrez, Newcastle struggled in the Premier League and were ultimately relegated to the Championship. Shearer resigned as manager soon after, having won just one of his eight games in charge.

The challenges facing Shearer at Newcastle were significant. The club was in financial trouble, having been saddled with heavy debts by the previous owner, Mike Ashley. The squad was also in need of major overhaul, with a number of players past their prime. Shearer had to deal with a number of injuries to key players, including Michael Owen and Mark Viduka, and was unable to find a settled team.

Another challenge for Shearer was the lack of experience he had as a manager. Although he had worked as a pundit and had coached the England under-21 team for a brief period, he had never managed a club before. This lack of experience showed at times, as Shearer struggled to motivate his players and get the best out of them.

Despite the disappointment of relegation, Shearer's brief stint as Newcastle manager is remembered fondly by the club's fans. His love for the club and his passion for the game were evident throughout his time in charge, and his determination to keep the club in the Premier League was admirable.

After Shearer's short-lived tenure as manager, he returned to punditry and media work. He continued to voice his opinions on Newcastle's performances and the wider footballing world. However, in 2019, he made a surprise return to the club as a member of the board of directors. The move was welcomed by fans, who saw it as an opportunity to bring someone with such a deep connection to the club back into the fold.

In his role as a director, Shearer has been an advocate for the club and has worked to help improve its fortunes. He has been vocal in his support of the current manager, Steve Bruce, and has backed the club's signings and transfer decisions. He has also been involved in discussions about the development of the club's youth academy, and has worked to help bring in new talent.

Beyond his work with Newcastle, Shearer has continued to be a respected voice in the footballing world. He has provided insightful commentary and analysis on matches and players, and has been a regular fixture on television screens during major tournaments such as the World Cup and the European Championships.

Shearer's achievements both on and off the pitch have earned him widespread admiration and respect. He is regarded as one of the greatest strikers of his generation, and his commitment to Newcastle United has made him a legend among the club's fans. As he continues to work to help improve the fortunes of the club, his legacy as a player and a leader will continue to be celebrated.

Strategies to motivate and inspire players

Alan Shearer is widely regarded as one of the greatest strikers in the history of English football, and his successful playing career has helped him develop strategies to motivate and inspire players. During his time as a manager, Shearer used these strategies to great effect, helping his team to achieve impressive results on the pitch.

One of the key strategies used by Shearer to motivate his players was to build a strong sense of team spirit. He believed that a united team was much more effective than a group of individual players, and he worked hard to foster a sense of togetherness amongst his squad. To achieve this, Shearer encouraged his players to spend time together off the pitch, whether that was through team meals, social events or simply spending time together in the dressing room. By doing so, he was able to create a positive and supportive team culture that helped his players to perform to their full potential on the pitch.

Another strategy used by Shearer to motivate his players was to set clear goals and objectives. He believed that players performed best when they had a clear idea of what they were working towards, and he was careful to communicate his expectations to his squad. Whether it was targeting a specific number of goals, aiming for a particular league position, or focusing on a particular style of play, Shearer was always clear about what he wanted his players to achieve.

In addition to setting clear goals, Shearer also believed in giving his players the freedom to express themselves on the pitch. He recognized that football is a creative game, and that players perform best when they are allowed to use their natural skills and instincts. To this end, he was always willing to experiment with different formations and tactics, and he encouraged his players to take risks and try new things on the pitch.

Another important aspect of Shearer's motivational strategies was his focus on positivity and encouragement. He believed that positive reinforcement was much more effective than criticism and negativity, and he always looked for ways to praise and encourage his players, even when things weren't going well. This helped to build confidence and self-belief amongst his squad, which in turn helped them to perform better on the pitch.

Finally, Shearer recognized the importance of leading by example. As a former player himself, he understood the pressures and demands of professional football, and he was always willing to get involved on the training pitch and lead by example. This helped to earn the respect of his players, and it helped to inspire them to give their best effort on the pitch.

In conclusion, Alan Shearer's success as a player and a manager can be attributed in part to his ability to motivate and inspire his players. Through building team spirit, setting clear goals, encouraging creativity, focusing on positivity and leading by example, Shearer was able to get the best out of his squad, and his strategies offer valuable insights for aspiring managers looking to achieve early success in their careers.

Legacy as a player and manager

Alan Shearer is undoubtedly one of the greatest footballers England has ever produced. His achievements as a player and a manager have earned him a special place in the hearts of football fans around the world. In this chapter, we will take a closer look at Shearer's legacy both as a player and a manager.

Shearer's Playing Career

Shearer began his professional career at Southampton in 1988. He quickly established himself as a prolific goalscorer and attracted the attention of several top clubs. In 1992, he joined Blackburn Rovers for a then-record fee of £3.6 million. Shearer's impact at Blackburn was immediate, and he helped the club win the Premier League in the 1994-95 season.

In 1996, Shearer joined his boyhood club Newcastle United for a then-world record fee of £15 million. Shearer's goalscoring prowess continued at Newcastle, and he became the club's all-time leading goalscorer with 206 goals in 404 appearances. He also won the Premier League Golden Boot three times and was named the PFA Player of the Year twice.

Shearer also had a distinguished international career, scoring 30 goals in 63 appearances for England. He played in three major tournaments for his country, including the 1998

World Cup, where he scored five goals and won the Bronze Boot as the tournament's third-highest goalscorer.

Shearer's success on the pitch earned him numerous accolades and recognition. He was awarded an OBE in 2001 for his services to football and was inducted into the English Football Hall of Fame in 2004.

Shearer's Management Career

After retiring as a player in 2006, Shearer worked as a pundit for the BBC. In April 2009, he was appointed as the interim manager of Newcastle United for the final eight games of the Premier League season. Shearer was unable to save the club from relegation, but his passion and commitment to the cause were evident.

Shearer returned to punditry after his brief stint as Newcastle manager, but there was speculation that he would return to management at some point in the future. In 2017, he took on a coaching role with the England national team, working as an attacking coach under Gareth Southgate.

Shearer's Legacy

Alan Shearer's legacy as a player and manager is one of excellence, dedication, and passion for the game. He is widely regarded as one of the greatest strikers in the history of English football and a true legend of Newcastle United.

As a player, Shearer's goalscoring ability was unmatched, and his achievements on the pitch have earned him a place among the all-time greats. He is a role model for aspiring footballers, and his dedication and professionalism both on and off the pitch set an example for others to follow.

Shearer's brief stint as Newcastle manager may not have resulted in on-field success, but his commitment to the club and his passion for the game left a lasting impression on the fans. He showed that he was willing to step up and take on a challenge, even if the odds were stacked against him.

Overall, Alan Shearer's legacy is one of excellence, dedication, and passion for the game. His achievements both as a player and a manager will be remembered for years to come, and he will continue to inspire generations of football fans and players around the world.

Chapter 7: Shearer's English Contemporaries
Steven Gerrard's early success at Rangers

Steven Gerrard, a former Liverpool and England captain, was appointed as the manager of Scottish club Rangers in May 2018. He arrived with no previous managerial experience, but his status as one of the greatest players of his generation and his leadership qualities made him an attractive prospect for the Glasgow-based club. Gerrard inherited a team that had finished third in the Scottish Premiership the previous season, well behind their fierce rivals Celtic.

In his first season in charge, Gerrard made a number of astute signings, including Croatian defender Nikola Katic and English midfielder Ryan Kent, and led the team to a second-place finish in the league, behind Celtic. He also guided Rangers to the group stages of the Europa League, where they finished third in a group that included Villarreal, Rapid Vienna, and Spartak Moscow.

However, it was in his second season in charge that Gerrard really began to make his mark. Rangers started the season strongly, winning their first four league games and qualifying for the group stages of the Europa League once again. Gerrard's side also made it to the final of the Scottish

League Cup, where they were narrowly defeated by Celtic in a penalty shootout.

Despite the disappointment of that defeat, Rangers continued to impress in the league, and by the end of the season they had closed the gap on Celtic considerably. Gerrard's side won 21 of their 30 league games, losing just four, and finished just two points behind Celtic in the final standings. They also reached the quarter-finals of the Europa League, where they were knocked out by German side Bayer Leverkusen.

Gerrard's impact on Rangers has been significant. His side plays with a high-intensity pressing game and has become much more defensively sound under his leadership. He has also given young players the chance to shine, with the likes of Ryan Kent, James Tavernier, and Alfredo Morelos all thriving under his tutelage.

Off the pitch, Gerrard has also made a big impact at Rangers. He has helped to rebuild the club's infrastructure and has established a positive culture within the dressing room. He has also been outspoken on a number of social issues, including racism and mental health, and has used his platform as Rangers manager to try and make a positive difference in the wider world.

Looking ahead, Gerrard will be hoping to guide Rangers to their first Scottish Premiership title since 2011. He will face tough competition from Celtic and other challengers, but the progress that he has made in his first two seasons in charge has given Rangers fans cause for optimism. Gerrard's early success at Rangers has shown that he has the potential to become one of the best managers of his generation and has cemented his place as a legendary figure in the history of English football.

Sol Campbell's short stint at Macclesfield Town

Sol Campbell is a former England international footballer who played as a centre-back. He is widely regarded as one of the best defenders of his generation, having won numerous domestic and international titles during his career. After retiring from professional football in 2011, Campbell took a break from the sport before deciding to pursue a career in football management. In 2018, he was appointed as the manager of Macclesfield Town, a small club in the fourth tier of English football. However, his time at the club was short-lived and ultimately ended in disappointment.

Background

After retiring from football, Campbell decided to take a break from the sport and pursue other interests. He worked as a pundit for various television channels, wrote for newspapers, and even studied for a degree in interior design. However, he always had a passion for football and wanted to get back into the game in a management role. In November 2017, Campbell completed his UEFA Pro Licence, the highest coaching qualification in European football, which gave him the credentials to manage a professional football team.

Appointment at Macclesfield Town

In November 2018, Campbell was appointed as the manager of Macclesfield Town, a club struggling in the fourth tier of English football. The club was facing financial difficulties and had been deducted points earlier in the season for failing to pay its players on time. Campbell was seen as a high-profile appointment, given his playing career and coaching credentials. However, his appointment was met with some skepticism due to his lack of experience in football management and the difficult circumstances surrounding the club.

Early success

Campbell's tenure at Macclesfield Town got off to a promising start, as he oversaw a run of four games without defeat. He quickly implemented a more defensive style of play and focused on improving the team's discipline and work ethic. Under his guidance, the team began to climb the table and picked up some impressive results against more established clubs. In January 2019, the club was awarded a £10,000 prize for being the most improved team in the EFL over the previous month.

Off-field challenges

Despite the team's improved performances on the pitch, Campbell faced numerous challenges off the field. The club's financial problems continued, and there were reports that players had not been paid for several weeks. Campbell also struggled to attract new players to the club due to its low budget and limited resources. In addition, he clashed with the club's board over the appointment of a new assistant manager and the allocation of funds for player transfers.

Relegation and departure

Despite Campbell's best efforts, Macclesfield Town was unable to avoid relegation from the Football League at the end of the 2018/19 season. The club finished 22nd in the table, five points adrift of safety. Despite this disappointment, Campbell remained committed to the club and began preparations for the following season. However, in August 2019, he resigned from his position as manager, citing a lack of support and resources from the club's board. His departure was seen as a blow to the club, which was once again facing a difficult season in the fourth tier of English football.

Conclusion

Sol Campbell's short stint at Macclesfield Town was a mixed experience. While he achieved some early success with the team and showed promise as a manager, he faced numerous challenges off the field and was ultimately unable to keep the club in the Football League. His departure from the club was seen as a setback for his coaching career, but he remains a respected figure in English football and is likely to pursue further opportunities in management in the future.

Ryan Lowe's promotion with Plymouth Argyle

Ryan Lowe is a former English professional footballer who played as a striker for various clubs in the Football League. After retiring from playing, Lowe began his coaching career, first as an assistant manager at Bury, before being appointed as the manager of Plymouth Argyle in June 2019. In his first season in charge, Lowe led the club to promotion from League Two to League One. This subtopic will examine Lowe's journey as a manager and his impact at Plymouth Argyle.

Background and Early Career

Born on September 18, 1978, in Liverpool, Ryan Lowe started his professional playing career at Burscough in 1998. He played for several clubs in the lower tiers of English football, including Shrewsbury Town, Chester City, Crewe Alexandra, Bury, and Tranmere Rovers. Lowe was known for his scoring ability and finished as the top scorer for his team in several seasons.

After retiring from playing in 2018, Lowe began his coaching career as the assistant manager of Bury. In March 2019, he was appointed as the caretaker manager following the departure of manager Ryan Lowe. However, after a successful stint as caretaker manager, Lowe was appointed as the permanent manager of Bury's League Two rivals Plymouth Argyle in June 2019.

Promotion with Plymouth Argyle

Lowe's first season at Plymouth Argyle was a successful one. He brought in several new players, including striker Joel Grant, midfielder Antoni Sarcevic, and defender Scott Wootton, and implemented a possession-based playing style. Despite a slow start to the season, the team picked up momentum and went on an unbeaten run of 14 games from November 2019 to January 2020. They also reached the fifth round of the FA Cup, where they were eventually knocked out by Premier League side Sheffield United.

The season was ultimately curtailed due to the COVID-19 pandemic, with Plymouth Argyle finishing in third place in League Two. However, the English Football League decided to use a points-per-game system to determine final standings, which saw Plymouth Argyle promoted to League One along with Crewe Alexandra and Swindon Town.

Impact at Plymouth Argyle

Lowe's impact at Plymouth Argyle went beyond just winning matches. He transformed the club's playing style and made it more attractive to fans. His team played with a possession-based approach, with an emphasis on quick passing and attacking football. Lowe also showed faith in young players, giving debuts to several academy graduates and promoting them to the first team.

Off the field, Lowe was praised for his man-management skills and his ability to build team spirit. He created a positive atmosphere around the club, which helped to motivate the players and improve their performance on the pitch.

Future Prospects

Following Plymouth Argyle's promotion to League One, Lowe signed several new players, including midfielder Lewis Macleod, defender James Wilson, and striker Frank Nouble, in an effort to strengthen the squad for the higher level of competition. The team started the 2020-21 season well, but a dip in form in the second half of the season saw them finish in 18th place, just three points above the relegation zone.

Despite the disappointing finish, Lowe's reputation as a promising young manager remains intact. He has shown that he has the ability to build a successful team and implement a playing style that suits his players. His man-management skills and positive approach have also been praised by players and fans alike.

Looking ahead, Lowe and his team will be focused on the challenge of competing in League One. They will face tougher opposition and will need to continue to develop their playing style and tactics to remain competitive.

One area that Lowe will be looking to improve upon is the team's defensive record. While Plymouth scored the second-most goals in the league, they also conceded a significant number of goals. This is an area that will need to be addressed if they are to compete at the higher level.

Another challenge for Lowe will be to retain key players and continue to bring in quality signings. With the success of the previous season, Plymouth's players will undoubtedly attract interest from other clubs, and it will be up to Lowe and his team to convince them to stay.

Off the pitch, Lowe has also made an impact on the club and the community. He has been involved in various initiatives to support the local community and has helped to strengthen the relationship between the club and its fans. This has helped to create a positive atmosphere around the club, which has undoubtedly contributed to the team's success.

Overall, Ryan Lowe's promotion with Plymouth Argyle was a significant achievement and a testament to his abilities as a manager. He has shown that he has the potential to become a successful manager in the future and has already attracted attention from other clubs. For now, he will be focused on the challenge of competing in League One and continuing to build upon the success of the previous season.

Graham Potter's rise at Swansea City

Graham Potter's journey from a lower-league player to a highly-rated manager is one of the most fascinating stories in English football. After retiring from playing at the age of 30, Potter embarked on a coaching career that saw him take charge of teams in Sweden, before eventually landing the Swansea City job in 2018.

The appointment of Potter came at a difficult time for Swansea City. The club had just suffered relegation from the Premier League and there was a sense of uncertainty around the club. Potter's appointment was seen as a gamble, but the Swansea hierarchy was impressed with his work in Sweden and believed he could take the club forward.

Potter's first season at Swansea was a mixed one. The team played some good football and finished in mid-table, but there were concerns that the squad lacked the necessary quality to challenge for promotion. However, Potter's approach to the game and his ability to get the best out of his players impressed the fans and the board.

The 2019-20 season saw Potter lead Swansea to the brink of the playoffs, but a late dip in form saw the team finish in mid-table. However, the season was seen as a success by many, with Potter's side playing an attractive brand of football and showing signs of progress.

Potter's playing style is based on possession-based football and an emphasis on developing young players. He has shown a willingness to experiment with different formations and is not afraid to make bold tactical decisions. His ability to motivate his players and get the best out of them has been praised by his peers and players alike.

One of the highlights of Potter's time at Swansea has been his work with young players. He has given opportunities to several academy players and has been credited with developing some of the most exciting talents in the Football League. The likes of Daniel James and Joe Rodon have gone on to make big-money moves to the Premier League, while the likes of Connor Roberts and Ben Cabango have become key players for Swansea.

Potter's success at Swansea has not gone unnoticed, and in the summer of 2019, he was linked with a move to Premier League side Brighton & Hove Albion. After weeks of speculation, Potter eventually made the move to the south coast and took charge of Brighton ahead of the 2019-20 season.

Potter's first season at Brighton was a challenging one, with the team battling relegation for much of the campaign. However, the team showed signs of improvement towards the end of the season, and Potter's tactical approach and man-management skills were praised by the club's hierarchy.

The 2020-21 season saw Brighton improve significantly, with the team playing an attractive brand of football and finishing in a respectable 16th place. Potter's approach to the game and his ability to develop young players were once again in evidence, with the likes of Tariq Lamptey and Yves Bissouma impressing under his guidance.

Potter's rise to prominence in English football has been impressive, and he is now regarded as one of the most promising young managers in the game. His ability to develop young players and his willingness to experiment with different tactical approaches have earned him many admirers, and it is clear that he has a bright future ahead of him.

Potter's success at Swansea did not go unnoticed, and he was soon approached by Premier League club Brighton & Hove Albion in May 2019. He signed a four-year contract with the club and was tasked with keeping them in the Premier League, which he accomplished in his first season in charge. Despite finishing 15th in the league, Potter's impact on the club was evident, and many praised his attacking style of play.

In his second season at Brighton, Potter continued to impress, earning a reputation for his tactical flexibility and willingness to adapt his team's approach to different opponents. Brighton's performances improved, and they finished the season in 16th place, five points clear of the relegation zone. Potter's emphasis on developing young players was also evident, with the likes of Ben White, Tariq Lamptey, and Aaron Connolly becoming key players in the squad.

Potter's success at Brighton has earned him recognition as one of the brightest managerial talents in English football. His willingness to take on a difficult challenge and his ability to implement his vision for the team have been praised by many. He has also shown a willingness to engage with fans and the media, often discussing his tactical decisions and providing insight into his thought process.

One of the most impressive aspects of Potter's management style is his willingness to adapt and experiment with different tactics and formations. He has used a variety of systems at Brighton, including a back three, a back four, and a midfield diamond. He has also been willing to play players out of position, using wing-backs and central defenders in midfield roles to great effect.

Potter's emphasis on possession-based football and his ability to develop young players have drawn comparisons to former Arsenal manager Arsene Wenger. Like Wenger, Potter places a great emphasis on the technical abilities of his players and believes in playing an attacking brand of football. He has also been praised for his ability to spot young talent, with many of the players he has developed going on to have successful careers in the Premier League.

Overall, Graham Potter's rise at Swansea and subsequent success at Brighton has established him as one of the most promising young managers in English football. His tactical flexibility, willingness to experiment, and emphasis on developing young players have earned him many admirers, and it is clear that he has a bright future ahead of him. If he continues to progress at the same rate, it may not be long before he is managing one of the biggest clubs in the game.

Conclusion
The common factors contributing to early success in management

Aspiring young managers are always on the lookout for success stories to learn from and emulate. While each manager's path to success is unique, there are common factors that contribute to early success in management. In this section, we will examine some of these factors and what aspiring young managers can learn from them.

1. Clear vision and philosophy: One of the most important factors contributing to early success in management is having a clear vision and philosophy for how the team should play. Successful managers like Jurgen Klopp, Pep Guardiola, and Mauricio Pochettino all have a clear playing style and philosophy that they instill in their teams. They are able to communicate this vision effectively to their players and get them to buy into it. Aspiring young managers should develop a clear vision for how they want their team to play and work to implement it effectively.

2. Attention to detail: Successful managers pay close attention to every detail, from training sessions to match preparation. They analyze opposition teams and develop strategies to exploit their weaknesses. They also work tirelessly to improve their own team's weaknesses. Attention

to detail is essential for success in management, and aspiring young managers should work hard to develop this skill.

3. Man-management skills: The ability to manage people effectively is another key factor contributing to early success in management. Managers who are able to create a positive team culture and foster strong relationships with their players are often more successful than those who do not. Aspiring young managers should work on developing their man-management skills, learning to motivate and inspire their players.

4. Adaptability: Football is a constantly evolving game, and successful managers are those who are able to adapt to changing circumstances. They are willing to experiment with different tactical approaches and make changes to their team when necessary. Aspiring young managers should be willing to adapt their tactics and approach to the game based on their team's strengths and weaknesses.

5. Patience and perseverance: Finally, early success in management is not always immediate, and it often takes time to build a successful team. Successful managers like Eddie Howe and Julian Nagelsmann have shown patience and perseverance in their approach, sticking to their vision and philosophy even in the face of setbacks. Aspiring young

managers should be patient and persevere in their approach, working steadily towards their goals.

In conclusion, early success in management is a combination of many factors, including a clear vision and philosophy, attention to detail, man-management skills, adaptability, and patience and perseverance. Aspiring young managers should work to develop these skills and apply them in their approach to the game. By learning from the success stories of managers like Klopp, Guardiola, and Nagelsmann, and applying these lessons to their own approach, they can increase their chances of achieving success in management.

Lessons for aspiring young managers

Aspiring young managers can learn many lessons from the careers of the managers discussed in this book. While each manager had a unique journey and faced different challenges along the way, there are several key themes that emerge from their stories that can be helpful to those looking to follow in their footsteps.

One of the most important lessons is the importance of hard work and perseverance. All of the managers in this book faced setbacks and challenges at various points in their careers, but they never gave up. Instead, they continued to work hard and pursue their goals, even in the face of adversity. This persistence and determination helped them to overcome obstacles and achieve success.

Another important lesson is the need to be adaptable and willing to learn. The game of football is constantly evolving, and successful managers need to be able to adapt to new trends and tactics. This requires a willingness to learn from others and to experiment with new ideas. Many of the managers in this book were successful in part because they were open-minded and willing to try new things.

Effective communication is another important skill for aspiring managers. Whether it's communicating with players, staff, or the media, successful managers need to be able to get their message across clearly and effectively. They also need to be good listeners, able to take feedback from others and incorporate it into their decision-making.

A strong work ethic is also essential for success as a manager. The best managers are those who are willing to put in the time and effort needed to achieve their goals. This includes not only working with the team on the training ground and during matches but also spending time analyzing opponents, studying game footage, and building relationships with key stakeholders.

Finally, it's important for aspiring managers to understand that success in football is not just about results on the pitch. It's also about building a strong team culture, establishing good relationships with players and staff, and maintaining a positive public image. Successful managers need to be able to balance these different priorities and to lead their team with a clear sense of purpose and direction.

In conclusion, the stories of the managers discussed in this book provide valuable lessons for aspiring young managers. Hard work, perseverance, adaptability, effective communication, a strong work ethic, and a focus on building a positive team culture are all key ingredients for success in the world of football management. By learning from the experiences of these successful managers, young coaches can increase their chances of achieving their own goals and making a name for themselves in the game.

Future prospects for young managers in football

Football is a constantly evolving sport, and the landscape of management is no exception. As we have seen in this book, there are numerous examples of young managers who have achieved early success and earned recognition for their achievements. However, it is important to consider what the future holds for young managers in football.

One of the most significant changes in recent years has been the increasing role of data analytics in football management. As technology continues to advance, it is likely that data analysis will become even more important in shaping the game. This presents both opportunities and challenges for young managers. On the one hand, those who are able to effectively utilize data analysis tools and techniques may have a significant advantage over their peers. On the other hand, there is a risk that over-reliance on data could stifle creativity and innovation.

Another key factor to consider is the growing importance of mental health in football. As the sport becomes more competitive and demanding, there is a greater awareness of the pressures and stresses faced by players and managers alike. This has led to a greater focus on mental health support, and it is likely that this trend will continue in the future. Young managers who are able to prioritize the mental wellbeing of their players and create a positive team culture may find themselves at an advantage.

In addition, there is the ongoing issue of diversity and inclusion in football. The lack of representation of minority groups in management is a significant issue, and there is a growing recognition of the need to address this. Young managers who are able to demonstrate a commitment to diversity and inclusion may find themselves better equipped to navigate this changing landscape.

Of course, there are also broader trends and challenges that will shape the future of football management. The ongoing impact of the COVID-19 pandemic, the changing economics of the sport, and the increasing influence of social media are just a few examples. However, what is clear is that young managers who are able to adapt to these changes and demonstrate a strong understanding of the sport and its culture will have the best chance of achieving long-term success.

In conclusion, the future prospects for young managers in football are both exciting and uncertain. While there are numerous opportunities for those who are able to adapt and innovate, there are also significant challenges to be faced. By focusing on key areas such as data analysis, mental health, and diversity, young managers can position themselves to succeed in this constantly evolving landscape. Ultimately, it will be those who are able to balance innovation with tradition, and demonstrate a deep understanding of the sport and its culture, who will be best positioned to achieve long-term success in football management.

Key Terms and Definitions

To help you better understand the language and concepts related to aging and older adults, below you will find a list of key terms and their definitions.

1. Football manager: A person who is responsible for the tactical and strategic direction of a football team, including player selection, training, and game management.

2. Young manager: A football manager who is relatively young in age and/or new to the profession.

3. Success: In the context of football management, success can be defined as achieving positive results on the pitch, such as winning matches, trophies, or promotions, as well as developing players and implementing a successful playing style.

4. Promotion: The act of a football team moving up to a higher division or league, usually as a result of finishing in a high position in the previous season.

5. Relegation: The act of a football team moving down to a lower division or league, usually as a result of finishing in a low position in the previous season.

6. Tactical approach: The strategy or game plan a football manager employs in order to achieve success on the pitch, often taking into account the strengths and

weaknesses of their own team as well as those of their opponents.

7. Player development: The process of improving the skills and abilities of individual football players, often through targeted training and coaching.

8. Man-management: The ability of a football manager to effectively communicate with and motivate their players, as well as handle interpersonal relationships within the team.

9. Playing style: The particular way a football team approaches the game, often influenced by the manager's tactical approach, as well as the strengths and weaknesses of the team's players.

10. Legacy: The impact and lasting impression a football manager leaves on a team or the wider football community, often measured by their success, innovation, or contribution to the development of the game.

11. Tactical flexibility: The ability of a team or manager to adapt their tactics and formation to suit different opponents and situations.

12. Player development: The process of improving the skills, physical fitness, and mental strength of individual players through coaching, training, and mentoring.

13. Man-management: The ability of a manager to build positive relationships with players, motivate them, and handle interpersonal conflicts effectively.

14. Club culture: The shared values, traditions, and expectations that shape the identity and behavior of a football club and its stakeholders.

15. Recruitment strategy: The process of identifying and acquiring new players that fit the team's playing style, budget, and long-term goals.

16. Financial sustainability: The ability of a club to balance its revenues and expenses over the long term, without relying on external funding or risking bankruptcy.

17. Football philosophy: The underlying principles and beliefs that guide a team's playing style, approach to training, and overall strategy.

18. Performance analysis: The use of data and statistics to evaluate a team's performance, identify areas for improvement, and inform tactical decisions.

19. Pressure management: The ability of a manager to handle the high-pressure and high-stakes nature of professional football, including media scrutiny, fan expectations, and the risk of job loss.

20. Leadership: The ability of a manager to inspire, guide, and motivate a team towards a shared goal, while also making tough decisions and taking responsibility for results.

Supporting Materials

Introduction:
- Kuper, S. (2018). Soccernomics (rev. ed.). Nation Books.

Chapter 1: Jose Mourinho
- Clegg, J., & Riley, C. (2013). The Numbers Game: Why Everything You Know About Football Is Wrong. Penguin.
- Caioli, L. (2015). Mourinho: The Special One. Icon Books.
- Jose Mourinho: The Rise of the Translator. (2015). Documentary. Directed by Barney Douglas.

Chapter 2: Brendan Rodgers
- Rodgers, B. (2018). Brendan Rodgers: The Road to Paradise. Penguin UK.
- Wilson, J. (2013). Behind the Curtain: Travels in Eastern European Football. Orion.
- Cox, M. (2016). Zonal Marking: From Ajax to Zidane, the Making of Modern Soccer. Nation Books.

Chapter 3: Julian Nagelsmann
- Cox, M. (2018). The Mixer: The Story of Premier League Tactics, from Route One to False Nines. HarperCollins.
- Honigstein, R. (2018). Das Reboot: How German Football Reinvented Itself and Conquered the World. Nation Books.
- White, J. (2018). The Coach: Lessons on the Game of Life. Constable.

Chapter 4: Nagelsmann's German Contemporaries

- Uersfeld, S. (2019). Building the Yellow Wall: The Incredible Rise and Cult Appeal of Borussia Dortmund. Weidenfeld & Nicolson.
- Winkler, M. (2019). Klopp: Bring the Noise. Crux Publishing.
- Hytner, D. (2020). Bayern Munich: Creating a Global Superclub. Bloomsbury Sport.

Chapter 5: Eddie Howe

- Winton, R. (2018). Eddie Howe: The Man Who Changed Football. DeCoubertin Books.
- Wilson, J. (2015). The Outsider: A History of the Goalkeeper. Bloomsbury Sport.
- Cox, M. (2014). The Mixer: The Story of Premier League Tactics, from Route One to False Nines. HarperCollins.

Chapter 6: Alan Shearer

- Shearer, A. (2016). Alan Shearer: My Life in Football. Headline.
- Rich, T. (2015). The Biography of Tottenham Hotspur: The Incredible Story of the World Famous Spurs. Kings Road Publishing.
- Cox, M. (2017). Zonal Marking: The Making of Modern European Football. HarperCollins.

Chapter 7: Shearer's English Contemporaries

- Lowe, J. (2019). The Adventures in the Debris of the World Cup. Bloomsbury Sport.
- Taylor, D. (2019). The Anatomy of Liverpool: A History in Ten Matches. Orion.
- Cox, M. (2018). The Mixer: The Story of Premier League Tactics, from Route One to False Nines. HarperCollins.

Conclusion:
- Goldblatt, D. (2015). The Game of Our Lives: The Meaning and Making of English Football. Nation Books.
- Cox, M. (2019). published.
- Clegg, J., & Riley, C. (2018). The The Tactical Side of Pep Guardiola, Jurgen Klopp, and Mauricio Pochettino. Independently Mixer: The Story of Premier League Tactics, from Route One to False Nines. HarperCollins.

www.ingramcontent.com/pod-product-compliance
Lightning Source LLC
LaVergne TN
LVHW012121070526
838202LV00056B/5820